T0194925

Discovering
Who I Am

SHONDOLYN LATHAM

authorHOUSE®

AuthorHouse™
1663 Liberty Drive
Bloomington, IN 47403
www.authorhouse.com
Phone: 1 (800) 839-8640

Published by AuthorHouse 08/02/2019

ISBN: 978-1-7283-2122-6 (sc)
ISBN: 978-1-7283-2121-9 (e)

Library of Congress Control Number: 2019910648

Print information available on the last page.

I have always enjoyed writing. Never realizing that this was my passion. Now that I'm older I can tell you that those childhood dreams and ambitions never leave your mind. Everyone has a gift. When I was the kid I didn't like getting in trouble. I made sure to do all that was required of me so that I wouldn't get in trouble. Sometimes I fell short and did get in trouble. In school most of the time the class would get in trouble as a whole for talking. When I was younger, I remember being in elementary school doing a quiet celebration in my head (because I loved to write) when the teacher made the whole class write one sentence over and over again for being disobedient. Usually the sentence would say; I will not talk in class. We had to write that sentence as many times as the teacher requested. 250 to 500 times was the average. I know it was weird to enjoy the class punishment as much as I did. But I did. Back then I knew I enjoyed writing I just didn't know what to write about. Today I still enjoy writing, and now I have a story to write about.

Going through this journey called life, I have realized that events happen throughout your life set you up to live in your purpose. Some people discover their purpose early in life, some later, and some never get the opportunity to discover their's. I am very fortunate to be able to step back, take a look at my life, and realize that way back then I was placed on this earth to one day tell my story. I was raised on a strong foundation. My great grandfather was a strong country man. He was a farmer. We never had to go to the store to buy fruit, veggies, and sometimes meat. He grew plenty of fruit and veggies. And raised animals. When granddad tilled the ground we walked behind him picking up giant globs of dirt sometimes throwing them at him. He never said anything he just kept farming. I never heard grandad raise his voice. He had his way of scaring us straight though. If he told you not to do something you better had listened, because he was gonna tell you a scary story to make you wish you had listened. The stories that he told seemed so real! Sometimes he would let us help him in the garden, but we would always do something devilish to make him put us out of the garden. I remember one time he was planting peas, and he let us help. We just took a hand full of the peas and threw them up in the air. When it was time to harvest the crop you could see the results of our devilish acts. Grand daddy instilled that strong work ethic in us. Teaching us that you had to work in order to have something. His dedication to hard work trends down throughout my family. His children; my grandma, great aunts, great uncles, their children; my mom, my aunts, their children; me my brothers, sister, and cousins. We all have that drive. Our family is big on faith and prayer. When things were rough praying always made it better. I never knew that I would have to lean so heavily on my faith to help me through my life. In many situations my faith in Jesus Christ was all I had. One scripture that plays over and over in my head is; Hebrews Chapter 11:1. And it reads NOW FAITH IS THE SUBSTANCE OF THINGS HOPED FOR, THE EVIDENCE OF THINGS NOT SEEN. I don't want to make it seem like my family was perfect because we weren't and still aren't. Along the way I have made a lot of wrong decisions and chose wrong career paths, but God always bring me back to writing. Whether it's through journaling or trying to go back to school to Pursue a degree. There have been several instances where my life was soooo hard. Divorced in 1994, being evicted twice, and coming home from a years stay in Memphis and discovering that the apartment complex had taken my 1st car that I finished paying for to the pound. It was on a flat and the tag had expired. Things just kept hitting me in my face seemingly year after year. On top of continued turmoil, my son having a life threatening illness, I loose my home in 2016. I did a lot of journaling. I wasn't writing about anything in particular. I guess you can say I was writing about something. The most significant and meaningful thing that anybody could write. I was journaling my prayers. I was stressed to the point that I was having trouble making it to my work station daily. I was so dizzy and off balance. I didn't share that with many people. I did have one friend to walk with me daily to make sure that I got to my office ok. Once I got into my office, I would pull out my personal journal and start praying while writing it on paper. The following prayers are just a few of many. This really helped and I enjoyed it.

My Prayer Journal

Lord, I need to talk to You.

This Journal Belongs to:

Shandolyn   Latham

Thank you Lord for this Day. Jesus
I need you, I love you Lord. Lord
Jesus I'm just feeling overwhelmed
with thanks giving Lord. You
have been my and still are my
Strength, my help, my life
Lord. I thank you Sr. Lord
Show me your right Jesus. I
need you Lord everyday. Every
hour every minute. Glory
Second Jesus. Hallelujah Lord
Thank you Jesus. Keep us
Lord. Bless us in Our Strength
+ our Quest for you Jesus.
Lord I thank you, I love you
Jesus.
Heal All Sickness
Jesus In our
bodies, purity
Us Lord. Clean
us up Jesus.

> Lean on thyself until thy strength is
> tried; then ask God's help; it will not
> be denied. Use thine own sight to
> see the way to go; When darkness
> falls, ask God the path to show.
>
> *Ella Wheeler Wilcox*

Like Anthony Brown says
in his song worth, You thought
I was to die for, you sacrificed
your life so I can be freed

Thank
you

Jesus

I am always content with what happens; for I know that what God chooses is better than what I choose.

Epictetus

Thank you Lord for this day
thank you Lord for my health
and strength to push on when
I don't feel or want too.
I thank you Lord for being
in charge over my life.
Thank you for my family my
friends, my future husband Lord
Jesus you are Lord of Lords
+ King of Kings Jesus I just
thank you Sir. for All you
do. Keep us Lord in your
care bless my son Heal his
body Lord Remove all that
is not healthy Lord I ask
you to bless my son in
Alaska. God. keep him
strong Jesus Show him
How much strength he has
Start opening his eyes to
the blessings that he has
within himself. Be with my
Daughter Lord Please don't
Allow her to grow up to fast.
Keep her humble Jesus. +
pure. Protect her Jesus
Bless my Mom Lord Thank
you for her strength She makes
me be strong when I can't
Thank you for her. Thank
you Lord for my Brothers + Sis.

Thank you Jesus

Create in me a clean heart Jesus. Take out all impurites teach me how to love with only the love of you Jesus. Open my eyes to the true + pure things in life God Bless your people God in that they learn the Love of you + act on that Love so that this can be a better world. Keep us Jesus Protect us from All hurt harm + danger. Heal our bodies God of things all that shouldn't be, sickness doubt fear, Bless us Jesus And Help us walk in the way you would have us go.

Thank you Jesus

Thank you Jesus!!

Thank you Lord for this Day!
Jesus Thank you for keeping
us as we sleep. Lord I Just
thankyou for being You God. Jesus
I ask that you bless us
throughout this day. Jesus
Protect us from All hurt harm
and Danger. Any Assignment
that the devil has for our
lives Block in Lord Jesus.
Jesus I thankyou for my
family and friends. Jesus
As Always I'm Just thankful
for your mercy and Grace.
In Jesus P erhaps one reason God delays His
name I Pray answers to our prayers is
Fix all Situation because He knows we need to
for our Good be with Him far more than we
Lord I ask you need the things we ask of Him.
to watch over Ben Patterson
my family and
friends all over the world. Jesus
Pour an extra blessings toward
their way. Lord I ask you
to please help us to work
on our health and fitness
Jesus Help my son to loose
weight Jesus the Right way
and me as well. Lord Jesus I thank
you for my family Bless DJ
Kadence, Mom, My Sister Christine
and my Brothers Tyson + Dauayne
Bless my dad Lord. Bring us
all closer as a family in your
name Jesus.

May 17, 2021

Thank you Lord. Jesus you know my heart's desires Lord. I ask that you lead me down the correct path and enable me to go through the process to accomplish my goals. Thank you Jesus for all you do. I ask you Lord to lead + guide me in the way you would have me to go. Thank you Father for your grace + mercy. Be with my family Lord Bless us all Lord Jesus + Give us peace in the midst of the storm. Lord I just thank you.

Thank you Lord for this day.
Thank you Lord for waking us
in our right minds. Lord Jesus
I just come to you this morning
to say thankyou Jesus for
your grace & mercy Lord. Lord
Jesus I can't make it with
out you. Help me Lord. Creado
in me a righteous spirit &
a clean heart. Lord I can't
say this enough. I just thank
you Sir.

We wait in hope for the Lord; he is our help and our shield.

Psalm 33:20 NIV

Thank you Lord for this day. Yes Jesus you are our shield. Protect me Lord from All evil, and wrong doers. Keep me Jesus. Lord I just Ask you to be with me Lord Protect me from All hurt harm + Danger Protect my family + love ones I thank you Lord for strength Jesus. Thank you for All you do Lord I ask you to bless me in my goals Lord Jesus make a way for me to Achieve All that I desire that's going to be for the well being of my family And I Jesus I want to write a Book, I want to open my own Gym + fitness Center. I want to complete College. Help me Jesus! I just thank you in Advance + I thank you for process + progress

THANK YOU

JESUS

Thank you Lord for this day. Thank you for strength. Thank you Lord for watching over us as we slept last night. Jesus I come to you asking for piece in the mist of the storm. Lord I thank you for this solid foundation you have placed me on. Lord you held me get over the toughest obsticals and I just thank you Sir. Lord Bless my family Lead & Guide us all in the way you want us to go. Lord Again I thank you for Strength & Power

Thank you

Jesus.

We cannot abandon life because of its storms. The strongest trees are not found sheltered in the safety of the forest, rather they are in open spaces—bent and twisted by winds of all seasons. God provides deep roots when there are wide-spreading branches.

Tommy Felton

Dspite of my circumstances I still trust you lord. Jesus we need you. Lord I ask you to please watch over my son Lord I just pray you protect him. Heel his mind Lord. Bless him Jesus to hang on & give him strength through this storm. Jesus please make him whole after this storm renew his spirit his mind & his health. Lord God Give him Joy. Jesus I just pray for you to put your shield of protection around him

> What other nation is so great as to have their gods near them the way the LORD our God is near us whenever we pray to him?
> Deuteronomy 4:7 NIV

now Lord Jesus Let him know that I love him inspite of his mistakes & wrong Doings Jesus I Thank you for Life. Thank you Lord

Thank you Lord for this day. Thank you Lord for holding me close helping me to make through this journey of life. Lord I thank you for watching over me And my family as we all slept. God I ask you to pour a special Blessing upon my Children bless them Lord in All areas that are weak Build them up Jesus in their Health their Knowledge knowledge knowledge Knowledge Lord watch over them & keep them Safe Jesus pour a special Blessing upon all three of them. Jesus watch over Djaye Jesus keep him safe Lord Give him the ability to Keep a sound mind & Bless him As he Becomes more mature in you Jesus Give him wisdom & understanding bless Dejun Lord Heal his Body Jesus Be with my baby Lord Be with him Lord Bless Kadence Jesus heal her knees, Allow her Lord to Reach her full potential Keep her pure Jesus I pray Lord that you Bless All my Kids to Reach their full potential

Now that I'm older, wiser, and settled the idea of writing is still fascinating to me. So I Shondolyn Michelle have decided to share my story with the world..... Being the age I am, I never imagined waking up feeling like I'm struggling to know who I am. I've always thought that I knew myself just going through life the traditional way; waking up going to work everyday and coming home doing household duties like I've saw my hold life. I've tried several things and I would always quit doing whatever it was and begin something else. Most of the time it wasn't by choice. Devin would always get sick and I would stop whatever I had started. That was my obligation to him as a mother. That was the one thing that seemed to always be for certain to me. I was always going to do everything in my power to take care of him. Now that he's gone I'm having a hard time finding my place. I guess that's just the emotional side of me talking. Devin passed away on May 20, 2019. Even though he was ill, I was not expecting that!! Some would say because you have an ill child you should be able to handle the death a little easier, or you have a chance to prepare for the worst. Emotionally and physically drained especially over the last two years, I still had hope. As long as he was breathing there was hope. I was always praying for a miracle since day one of his diagnosis years ago. As the years went on those prayers got harder and stronger especially over the last two years. After he took his last breath, I stayed on his bed rubbing on him for over an hour. It was like I could see he was dead, but I was still hopeful that something just something could bring my baby back!! I always had hope and faith that he would get better. I thought that other events in my life were bad, but in reality The death of my precious son was the worst possible thing that I could have ever experienced!! It has changed so much in my life. I have to re-discover me. For a lot of years it seemed like My life was centered around him and his well being. Right now in this moment, I can truly say that my time with him seemed so short. I adored that little boy. I woke up and went to bed taking care of him before I even thought of doing anything else. I was living off of a schedule. And that schedule was based off of Devin's needs. I wanted him to live so bad!! At the same time I was trying to fit little pieces of what I wanted to do in some how. I tried to give myself at least one hour a day to do what I wanted to do. I chose exercising. Sometimes I didn't always get that hour, because my ultimate goal was to make sure he and my other two kids were ok.

If Devin had to be at appointments at anytime I was there. No matter when or where I had to travel. I would make arrangements for my other two children to be able to come to these appointments with us. I missed a lot of work and they missed a lot of school. I just enjoyed having them with me. Sometimes Devin's appointments were so frequent and so far away. All I knew was that I had to get him there. As a single mother that adores her children, I don't always do things because I want to. I do them because I have to. That's my responsibility to my children. Some parents don't have that drive for their children. I believe that some of those values have to be instilled in you at an early age. I saw my mom have to be so tough on so many occasions. I inherited that strength. Now I know how valuable that lesson was.

Unselfishness, Growth, Strength

Growing up I was a kind hearted soft spoken person. I never thought about myself first. I always put others feelings before mine. Some how I learned to be ok with others being ok before I was ok. I would always wait to get things if my mom ran short of money. I would let her buy for my younger siblings first. I would sometimes wait until her next pay day to get things. She always kept her word. Now that I'm older, I always said if I got it she got it. I love my mom so much. When I was a kid I wanted to always be in her presence. I birthed a clone of myself when I had Devin. He loved being around me. I felt bad when I had to send him to school or anywhere that separated us. He was a true momma's boy. I was a momma's girl. I was and I still am crazy about that lady. She sacrificed a lot for us.

I was so easy going, I kind of went with the flow all throughout my school years. Now that I think about it; I didn't want any attention placed on me. I just wanted to live day to day; never speaking my mind or putting myself in the spotlight. I was the oldest child of four. I had a big demand on me as the oldest sibling. That demand was to fill in when my mom couldn't. It kinda got overwhelming at times, but I did it. I remember one time one of my siblings called me momma and I got mad lol.

When I graduated high school I had a boyfriend, and I ended up getting married at nineteen. Thinking that that would give me a voice, but little did I know that only took me from the responsibilities of being a big sister to being something that I wasn't ready for; a wife! I never got a chance to be me. Or really know who I was. I still had the same responsibilities that I had at home but more. I had my first child at the age of 21. Then my next one at the age of 24. By the time my second son was one year old I was divorced and living alone trying to make it with two little boys. The drive and endurance that I saw in my mom, and the demand that she put on me was instilled in me. It made me a survivor through any circumstance. Giving me the ability to never cracked under pressure. Living in the moment and from day to day was my mindset. I would always have the drive to start something, but I would never finish. As the days passed I would end up losing interest in whatever I was trying to accomplish. It was a pattern. Looking through different lenses now, I realize that my unselfishness allowed me to stand in the shadow. I had patience to just wait my turn. Having Patience paid off while caring for Devin. I enjoyed his little spirit so much. His positive outlook on life. No matter what he faced he was always positive. Every morning he woke up with a smile on his face greeting Djaye, Kadence, and I with a Good Morning. He would always have a song in his heart. He displayed it through whistling while Opening curtains. A few of the words were; we are the salt of the earth. A bright light shining in a very dark world. While he's gone to prepare a place, we are the salt of the earth. If he wasn't whistling that he would be repeating the same phrase over and over again. "Ma it's a bright sunny day outside." My God I miss him so much!!

Having the responsibilities of being a mom I tried to make things work for me and my children, but financially I was never able to succeed. Every time I tried to survive on my own, I would end up moving back into my mom's home with my two babies. Momma was always there for me when nobody else was. I also had great support from my grandma for the short time she was able. My aunts helped me too when ever they could. When I didn't have it, if they had it I had it.

My grandma became very ill. So my mom took her in. My mom and my sister had left the home place and moved to Columbus. Momma left a trailer in Alabama. My brother, and I and my two babies stayed there. It wasn't long before I got overwhelmed again with life, and all its responsibilities. I had to move back in with my mom. Trying to go to school, work, raise two children, and help take care of my dying grandma was even more overwhelming. It seemed like every where I turned I was getting into situations that seemed impossible to endure. Now I see that I was being prepared for what was coming. I started experiencing dizziness, headaches, and short term memory loss. I was back and forth from doctor to doctor. One doctor put me on a pill at the age of 24 that was the same pill my dying grandma was taking; A nerve pill. I took that pill maybe two weeks. My other doctor seemed to have a little more compassion for his patients. So he told me that at 24 there was no need for me to be taking a nerve pill. He told me to fuel my body with proper nutrition and be sure to exercise.

After blacking out in class one day, and waking up to ambulance drivers closing the doors, My mom and a couple of my classmates from my college Cosmetology class told me I had a seizure. That was my first time having a seizure. So I thought. But come to find out those little short episodes of memory loss were possible seizures that hadn't been diagnosed. I just wasn't passing out. I would never tell anyone about the episodes I just kept that to myself. Soon I was put on a seizure medicine that made all of my symptoms stop. I didn't finish cosmetology school. I quit after I had the seizure there. I was afraid to go back. I didn't want to get sick there again. That was my second time blowing my chances to be a cosmetologist. I finished the course in high school, but didn't go take the state board test. In the process of me having seizures, my grandma passed away. That was the most hurtful thing I could ever experienced at that time. Grandma was my rock. School was put on the back burner again. I just wanted to feel better. Still a single mom. I would just work and take care of my children. I started exercising and drinking plenty of water finally like the doctor ordered. I found the water; especially cold water to be soothing to my body. The water and exercise paired, made me feel like I was beginning to live. Years of Moving in and out of my mom's house, I finally got a job that paid me enough money to where I could begin to stand on my own two feet. I got and apartment. I worked second shift. That was tough with two small children trying to get someone to stay with them at night. It was my life I had to make it work. I started this job in December of 1999. One day after my 29th Birthday on May 18, 2000 I found out that my baby boy had a brain tumor the size of a golf ball right between his optic nerves. I was shattered. There receiving this news alone, the doctors asked if I would be ok with what they were about to tell me. I told them yes I was ok. When they told me all I could say was Lord have mercy. That phrase seemed to get me through a lot of difficult times.

I'd noticed a problem with Devin's eyesight. I started taking him to eye doctors. After several eye doctors evaluated him, We ended up at Lebonheur children's hospital in Memphis, Tennessee. That day the MRI results confirmed that he had a brain tumor. We were admitted and scheduled for surgery the next day. I was 29, single, uprooted from my home, and placed in a whole new state that I've never been with a sick baby. I was an emotional wreck. The doctors did the surgery, and the next day came back into the room to tell me that the surgery was unsuccessful! They had to repeat the procedure! I was weak. I cried all night. I would always manage to pull it together or cry silently for Devin, because I never wanted him to see me broken. Sometimes he would know but he just wouldn't come out and say it. He would always say, "ma what you doing?" When I would answer him he would say, "your nose sounds stuffy." Lol he was so smart. My strength was his kryptonite. He was strong because he saw my strength. I couldn't let my strong little boy see me crack. He seemed to feed off of my energy. But to be honest, as courageous and strong as he was, I was feeding off of his energy. We were a team.

Still alone, single, and couldn't work. I was still in that living day to day mode. By this time I had mastered the day by day mentality. But now I was doing something different; I was fighting for the survival of my child. That quiet timid me was fading away. I had to fight, be observant, alert, and stand strong for my baby boy. I had no choice, but at the same time it was my honor to be there every step of the way. My son needed me like I've never been needed before. I knew meds and prescription strengths without looking at them. I knew what each med was for. The doctors had to explain ever medicine to me that they prescribed for Devin. If I saw physical change as a side effect from any of the medicine they would have to re-evaluate that medication, and find something that worked for Devin. The nurses had to recite the medicines and the dosage strengths to me before I allowed them to give them to my son. Some of the time they would leave one out or have the wrong dosage. Devin was so sweet and humble. I was going to give him the best possible me that I could give him. Becoming an advocate for him making sure everyone else gave him the same treatment. Everyone wasn't always so willing, but when they saw my passion for my child they quickly got on board.

I had to put everything on hold even my job, because Devin was admitted to A hospital that was hours away from home. My baby came first period. In the middle of all the chaos I became pregnant. On December 30th of 2001 I had a healthy baby girl. Still single, working when I could, and having three children I had to move back in with my mom. Lord momma was still there taking me in. Once I adapted to the lifestyle of having a sick child, I started trying to get some normalcy out of my not so normal life. Trying to do school again, but online this time; I struggled. I again Put it on the back burner. Eventually I finished that semester of online classes.

Now that Devin had become a patient at St. Jude Children's Hospital, I started to tell my children that we would treat the trips to St. Jude every three months like our own little vacations. It was fun for them and exhausting for me. Emotionally exhausted, I found joy in having all three of my babies with me. The hospital setting wasn't what I wanted, but Watching them play and getting involved with the numerous things that St. Jude offered gave me joy. Every clinic that Devin had to go to was like a playground for them. They had plenty to play with and plenty of children to play with. Every two years

Devin's tumor would return with a vengeance. Up rooting us from what was beginning to seem normal. But when I began to think about it, back and forth to the hospital was the norm for me and my children. I still had a desire to go to school, and when things seemed to get stable with Devin I re-enrolled in school online, but with a school in my hometown. The thing with this was that Exams had to be taken on the campus of the school. I was still a single mom, with three children now. Trying to make sure they were doing what they needed to do, and me taking college courses online, and attending classes in the mornings before work, I was making it happen. I was Still loving exercising and its benefits. I was walking five miles two days a week and doing cross fit through the week. I was jogging two miles non stop. I finally had my life together I thought. I was hit by a truck in the parking lot at work while walking to my car by a co- worker. My knee was injured. All that working out, and the big accomplishments that I made with my health was shattered. I was rushed to the hospital by ambulance. My mom, my brother Tyron, and my children Kadence and Devin were there when I got there. When they rolled me into the ER I saw my family and a few coworkers. I could hear the sniffles of Devin and Kadence. They were crying. I was ok so I thought. By the time I left the hospital I couldn't put any pressure on my right leg, and I was in a full leg brace for 6 weeks. I started to gain weight and after 11 years of being seizure free I had a seizure!! I found comfort in letting Devin get a feel of what it felt like to see someone else getting poked on and examined by doctors instead of him. But my little boy was such a momma's boy it was stressful on him. Once I got home he told us, "if one more thing bad happens I'm going to just burst out crying!" Lol when Devin spoke out he was fed up. He had that same spirit as I did. I birthed my twin when I had Devin. He thought of every one else's feelings before his own even though his health wasn't good. This little boy loved his momma just as I did mine. He was so loving. Even though he couldn't see, he saw through his emotions. He described my hugs as being warm and snuggly. Oh how I could use one of those warm snuggles from him right now. He made me view life through his eyes. It was so amazing. Everything was picture perfect no matter what the circumstances were.

Once I got settled and began to heal after the incident at work, Still in the full leg brace, a single mom, off work, and still taking online classes; It was time to take Devin back to St. Jude for a check up. He had a growing brain tumor again. We were uprooted and back to lebonheur hospital again. He had another brain surgery. The more surgeries he had the harder it was for him to recover. I started missing exams and eventually stopped school again. I was 45 credits in and only needed 65 credits total. My children are way more important than anything I could ever imagine doing for myself. I love my kids so much until it hurt me to even let them go to school. My babies missed sooo many days out of school. One because I always took them with Devin and I to Memphis and two I just enjoyed having them near me. As they got older I had to start making the trips to St. Jude alone just Devin and I. My daughter stayed home with my mom so that she could go to school. My oldest son Djaye was in the military. Devin and I made these trips for a while alone. He was so lonely without his little sister. She played with him all the time. It made him feel good to have someone to just play with him. Devin had to deal with so much in his health. I had to make sure everything else was perfect for him. He spent a lot of time with my daughter when she was a little girl. He literally molded her with his personality. They were playmates and best friends. Devin had his last surgery in October of 2017. That surgery took soooo much out of him. It took his smile, and most of his personality. He began to show visible signs of not being able to recover. I took him to St. Jude for physical and occupational therapy every week for a few months. When it was time for a check up in December of 2017 the doctors told me his tumor was back and it was really aggressive. They had given up on him. They told me that he may not make it to Christmas. Still a single mom I was distraught. Doctors never said that they had given up to me before. I was mixed with so many emotions. The two that were so strong was anger, and fear. I was angry at the doctors for not having anything else to offer my child, and feared for my sweet precious son's life!! When we left St. Jude, Devin had been placed on hospice. I struggled with the thought of putting him through more surgery so I knew it was time for me to let him help me make the decision. He never wanted to have brain surgery. So at this point I couldn't bare making that decision for him. I sat down and asked him if he wanted to have another brain surgery. He told me no. I asked him if he knew what would happen if he didn't. He told me, "yes I'm going to die." That pierced my soul to hear my sweet baby boy say that and sit there and seem comfortable with it. I was in tears, but at the same time I knew that it was time to honor his wishes. Still fighting for him as I always did. I kept taking him to the doctor, but I made the decision to keep it with his local doctors in our hometown. They had learned Devin and his condition. I was comfortable with letting them treat him with a strict watch over them by me. I missed a lot of work still and eventually I lost my home to foreclose. Again I had to move back in with my mom. Mom was still there. After a few months in her home, I found a home to rent. My son from the military came home. This was a rough year and the pressure wasn't letting up. Every few weeks I was taking Devin to the ER. He was getting sick more often. I decided to finally relax a little and start living a little. Traveling with my children. We went to Atlanta, Gadsden, Russellville, and Charlotte, North Carolina. All within a year. After a year it got hard for me to get Devin in and out of the house. So we didn't travel anymore. I saw a drastic decline in him and eventually he stopped eating by mouth. I had to get a feeding tube placed in his stomach in August of 2018. Shortly after that he stopped talking. We had a family dinner and took a family photo with my iPhone. That was the last picture with family that Devin was in. I was Unable to work, because now the local doctors had given up on him, and I had finally started to see it. I couldn't bare the thought of being at work and he pass away. So finally I had to start excepting reality, and I didn't want to keep exposing Devin to the negative comments of the doctors. I finally excepted hospice, and let them start coming into my home weekly to service Devin. On and off work I again as always fell into a bind financially. Thank God I had Landlords that were compassionate. They were so patient with me. People started to reaching out with financial support; My church, my job, and some family. I moved again into another home on March of 2019. It's bigger and it accommodated the needs of my family more. A bigger bed room for Devin and I to share. His bed and his supplies fit perfectly giving us both enough space. He was bed ridden. The bigger room allowed enough space for the nurses and aide to get in to assist Devin as needed. I started to go back to work and only leaving when I could hear the distress in my baby boy over the phone. That was pretty often. But my job was sooo amazing through this whole process with me and my son from day one way back in the year of 2000 up until the present. My birthday was coming up so I took May 17th through May 20th off for vacation. My vacation was being home and spending time with my kids. Devin had a horrible time that weekend. I was so emotional. I was so thankful that I had taken off work so that I could cater to him. I had told my family that Sunday night May 19th that I wasn't going back to work that Tuesday If Devin wasn't better. Unfortunately On May 20, 2019 at 9:40 P.M. I felt my baby boy breathe his last little gentle breath in my face. It was soooo soft and lite. He passed away!!! I could see it coming over the past two years, but My God I never expected it!! I had prayed sooo much for my son to live. At the five week mark of his death, that feeling of never finishing what I started has left me. I finally completed something that I started. My son's life had ended. A month before his 25th Birthday. And 19 years and 2 days after he was diagnosed with a cranialphringioma brain tumor. 3 days after my 48th Birthday I finally realize that I couldn't complete anything else because my assignment was to see my son through this. I finally finish something that I started. I've discovered who I am and my purpose!!! This assignment didn't leave me with a degree, but it left me with soooo much more. Endurance, strength, a voice, and finally I realize that my son's purpose here on earth was to get me out of the shadow and bring me out into the spotlight and let me shine. Let me shine for him. His death is still so brand new!! It still stings!!! The hurt is still so fresh!!! The tears are still flowing so heavily!!! My heart is still so broken!! Even in the mist of all this, I realize now that I have finally discovered who I am. I thank God for blessing me with Devin. His little short life carried such an impactful message for me. No matter how many times I had to start over, I realize that I never never let go of one project. And that was the well being and the fight for my baby boy. I missed him sooo much. Death is so final. It leaves you with no other choice but to pick yourself up and continue to press on. My sweet Devin!! It has been a total honor to be your momma! I am so blessed to have been chosen for that role. If I can get any comfort out of this experience, it will definitely be that God saw something special in me to assign you to me!! Thank you Jesus!!! To be honest I thought God was going to heal your little body here on earth so that I could witness it, but that was my will and not God's will. Baby boy you exited this life just as peacefully and humble as you lived it! There is noooooo doubt in my mind where you will live your eternal life. Heaven has been waiting on you!! I hope that you are having the time of your life walking those streets of gold being nosey with your new set of eyes and newly healed body. God allowed you to be an angel here on earth, and I can't express the gratitude that I feel because he allowed you to be in my household. I love you Devin. Thank you for the beautiful spirit that you brought into our lives and our home. Enjoy those beautiful wings baby boy!!! Kadence, Djaye, and I are having such a hard time living without you!!! Your assignment here on earth seemed so short!!! You taught me how to smile when I had no reason to smile, you taught me how to endure when I had no endurance, you taught me how to be strong when I had no strength, and you taught me how to fight when I had no fight in me!! The only thing that I'm not prepared to do is live without you!! Just know that I have enjoyed every moment of being your momma. I lost my earthly angel, but I gained a guardian angel. Saying I love you doesn't begin to express the love that I have for you! I miss you baby! ♥♥♥♥Love you always; Momma!!

RIH Devin!! ♥♥♥♥

About the Author

I was born in Alabama in a small town called Aliceville, and raised in Ethelsville, Alabama. I went to school in Carrollton Alabama both elementary and high school. I've dibbled and dabbled in college, with hopes of receiving several degrees in writing. I'm a daughter, a sister, a mom, but most of all I'm a strong woman. I'm quiet and soft spoken most of the time, but not afraid to speak my mind. I'm missed interpreted by a lot of people because I'm quite and I have such a solemn look lol. Most people that gets to know me and understands me definitely loves me. I love writing, exercising, and spending time with my children. Aside from writing, I'm a pretty girl. I love playing in makeup, getting my nails and feet done, etc. I've always dreamed of writing a book. Just the thought of putting my story on paper has always been fascinating to me. Now that I have accomplished it, my advice to everyone is to never give up on your dreams. No matter how long it takes, If you want it bad enough you can achieve it.

Printed in the United States
By Bookmasters